METRIC
& IMPERIAL
CONVERSIONS

ARMADILLO

ABBREVIATIONS

LENGTH / DISTANCE

mm	m/metre	=	millimetre
cm	c/metre	=	centimetre
dm	d/metre	=	decimetre
m		=	metre
km	k/metre	=	kilometre
in		=	inch
ft		=	foot

AREA

cm^2	=	square centimetres
m^2	=	square metres
ha	=	hectare

WEIGHT

g		=	gram
kg	k/gram	=	kilogram
oz		=	ounce
lb		=	pound

VOLUME

cu	=	cubic
fl oz	=	fluid ounces
cm^3	=	cubic centimetres
m^3	=	cubic metres

SPEED/TYRE PRESSURE

mph	=	miles per hour
kmh	=	kilometres per hour
Nm^2	=	Newton metres

2 CONVERSION FACTORS

To convert one measurement to another, multiply by figure shown:

Centimetres to inches	0.394
Metres to feet	3.281
Metres to yards	1.094
Kilometres to miles	0.621
cm^2 to sq inches	0.155
m^2 to sq feet	10.760
m^2 to sq yards	1.196
km^2 to sq miles	0.3861
Hectares to acres	2.471
km^2 to acres	247.105
cm^3 to cu inches	0.061
m^3 to cu feet	35.315
m^3 to cu yards	1.308
Litres to cu inches	61.030
Litres to pints	1.7598
Litres to gallons	0.199
Grams to ounces	0.0352
Grams to pounds	0.0022
Kilograms to pounds	2.205
Kilograms to tons	0.0009
Feet per min to mph	0.1134
kmh to mph	0.6213

3 COMMON MEASURES

LENGTH		IMPERIAL
1 mm	1 m/metre	0.039 in
10 mm	1 c/metre	0.39 in
10 cm	1 d/metre	3.94 in
100 cm	1 metre	39.37 in
1,000 m	1 kilometre	0.623 miles

AREA		IMPERIAL
1 mm^2	1 sq m/metre	0.0016 sq in
1 cm^2	1 sq c/metre	0.0155 sq in
100 cm^2	1 sq d/metre	15.500 sq in
1,000 cm^2	1 sq metre	10.764 sq ft
1,000 m^2	1 hectare	2.470 acres

VOLUME		IMPERIAL
1 cm^3	1 cu c/metre	0.061 cu in
100 cm^3	1 cu d/metre	61.024 cu in
1,000 dm^3	1 cu metre	35.315 cu ft

LIQUID VOL		IMPERIAL
1 l	1 litre	1.59 pints
100 l	1 hectolitre	22 gallons

WEIGHT		IMPERIAL
1 g	1 gram	0.0353 oz
1,000 g	1 kilogram	2.2046 lb
1,000 kg	1 tonne	0.9842 ton

4 — COMMON MEASURES

LENGTH

		METRIC
	1 inch	2.540 cm
12 inches	1 foot	30.480 cm
3 feet	1 yard	0.914 m
1,760 yards	1 mile	1.609 km

AREA

		METRIC
	1 sq inch	6.452 cm^2
144 sq in	1 sq foot	0.0929 m^2
9 sq feet	1 sq yard	0.836 m^2
4,840 sq yd	1 acre	0.405 ha
640 acres	1 sq mile	259 ha

VOLUME

		METRIC
	1 cu inch	16.387 cm^3
1728 cu inch	1 cu foot	0.028 m^3
27 cu feet	1 cu yard	0.765 m^3

LIQUID VOL

		METRIC
	10 fl ounces	0.284 litres
	1 pint	0.568 litres
2 pints	1 quart	1.136 litres
4 quarts	1 gallon	4.554 litres

WEIGHT

		METRIC
	1 ounce	28.3495 g
16 oz	1 pound	0.4536 kg
14 lb	1 stone	6.350 kg

INCHES	CM	CM	INCHES
1/8	0.318	1	0.394
1/4	0.635	2	0.788
3/8	0.953	3	1.12
1/2	1.27	4	1.576
5/8	1.588	5	1.970
3/4	1.905	6	2.364
7/8	2.220	7	2.758
1	2.540	8	3.152
2	5.108	9	3.546
3	7.620	10	3.940
4	10.16	11	4.334
5	12.700	12	4.728
6	15.240	14	5.516
7	17.78	16	6.304
8	20.32	18	7.092
9	22.86	20	7.88
10	25.400	22	8.668
16	40.640	24	9.456
20	50.8	26	10.244
30	76.2	28	11.032
40	101.6	30	11.820
50	127.0	40	15.760

6 LENGTH

FEET	METRES	METRES	FEET
1	0.305	1	3.281
2	0.611	2	6.562
3	0.914	3	9.843
4	1.219	4	13.124
5	1.524	5	16.405
6	1.829	6	19.686
7	2.134	7	22.967
8	2.384	8	26.248
9	2.743	9	29.529
10	3.048	10	32.810
20	6.096	20	65.520
30	9.144	30	98.430
40	12.192	40	131.240
50	15.240	50	164.050
100	30.480	100	328.100
200	60.960	200	656.200
300	91.440	300	984.300
400	121.880	400	1,312.400
500	152.400	500	1,640.500
1,000	304.800	1,000	3,281.000
2,000	609.800	2,000	6,562.000
5,000	1,524.000	5,000	16,405.000

7 DISTANCE

YARDS	METRES	METRES	YARDS
1	0.91	1	1.094
2	1.83	2	2.188
3	2.74	3	3.281
4	3.68	4	4.374
5	4.57	5	5.468
6	5.49	6	6.562
7	6.01	7	7.655
8	7.32	8	8.45
9	8.23	9	9.84
10	9.14	10	10.94
20	18.29	20	21.88
30	27.40	30	32.82
40	36.60	40	43.76
50	45.70	50	54.70
100	91.40	100	109.36
200	182.90	200	218.72
220	201.20	220	240.59
300	274.30	300	328.08
400	365.80	400	437.44
440	402.30	440	481.18
500	457.20	500	546.80
1,000	914.40	1,000	1,093.60
2,000	1,828.80	2,000	2,187.20
5,000	4,572.00	5,000	5,468.10

8 DISTANCE

MILES	KM	KM	MILES
1	1.61	1	0.62
2	3.38	2	1.24
3	4.83	3	1.86
4	6.44	4	2.49
5	8.05	5	3.11
6	9.65	6	3.73
7	11.26	7	4.35
8	12.87	8	4.97
9	14.48	9	5.59
10	16.09	10	6.20
20	32.18	20	12.40
30	48.27	30	18.64
40	63.36	40	24.86
50	80.45	50	31.07
60	96.54	60	37.28
70	112.63	70	43.50
80	128.72	80	49.71
90	144.81	90	55.93
100	160.90	100	62.14
500	804.70	500	310.70
1,000	1,609.33	1,000	621.40
2,500	4,023.40	2,500	1,553.40
5,000	8,046.70	5,000	3,106.90

9 CAPACITY

FL OZ	LITRES	LITRES	FL OZ
1	0.029	1	35.20
2	0.057	2	70.39
3	0.085	3	105.59
4	0.114	4	140.78
5	0.142	5	175.96
6	0.170	6	211.18
7	0.199	7	246.37
8	0.227	8	281.57
9	0.256	9	316.76
10	0.284	10	351.96
50	1.420	50	1,759.80
100	2.840	100	3,519.60

PINTS	LITRES	LITRES	PINTS
1	0.57	1	1.76
2	1.14	2	3.52
3	1.70	3	5.28
4	2.27	4	7.04
5	2.84	5	8.80
6	3.41	6	10.56
7	3.98	7	12.32
8	4.55	8	14.08
9	5.11	9	15.84
10	5.68	10	17.60
50	28.41	50	87.99
100	56.82	100	175.98

10 CAPACITY

GALLONS	LITRES	LITRES	GALLONS
1	4.55	1	0.22
2	9.09	2	0.44
3	13.64	3	0.66
4	18.18	4	0.88
5	22.73	5	1.10
6	27.28	6	1.32
7	31.82	7	1.54
8	36.37	8	1.76
9	40.91	9	1.98
10	45.46	10	2.20
11	50.01	11	2.42
12	54.55	12	2.64
13	59.10	13	2.86
14	63.64	14	3.08
15	68.19	15	3.30
16	72.74	16	3.52
17	77.28	17	3.74
18	81.83	18	3.96
19	86.37	19	4.18
20	90.92	20	4.40
25	113.65	25	5.50
50	227.30	50	11.00
75	340.96	75	16.50
100	454.60	100	22.00

DRY CAPACITY

BUSHELS	CU METRES	LITRES
1	0.037	36.4
2	0.074	72.7
3	0.111	109.1
4	0.148	145.5
5	0.184	181.8
10	0.369	363.7

CM^3	BUSHELS
1	27.50
2	55.00
3	82.50
4	110.00
5	137.00
10	275.00

LITRES	BUSHELS
1	0.027
2	0.055
3	0.082
4	0.110
5	0.137
10	0.275

12 VOLUME

CU INCHES	CM³	CM³	CU INCHES
1	16.39	1	0.061
5	81.94	5	0.305
10	163.87	10	0.610
20	327.74	20	1.220
50	819.36	50	3.050
100	1,638.71	100	6.100

CU FEET	M³	M³	CU FEET
1	0.03	1	35.32
5	0.14	5	176.58
10	0.28	10	353.15
20	0.57	20	706.30
50	1.42	50	1,765.80
100	2.83	100	3,531.50

CU YARD	M³	M³	CU YARD
1	0.76	1	1.31
5	3.82	5	6.54
10	7.65	10	13.08
20	15.29	20	26.16
50	38.23	50	65.40
100	76.46	100	130.80

13 WEIGHT

OUNCES	GRAMS		GRAMS	OUNCES
1	28.35		1	0.04
2	56.70		2	0.07
3	85.05		3	0.11
4	113.40		4	0.14
5	141.75		5	0.18
6	170.10		6	0.21
7	198.45		7	0.25
8	226.80		8	0.28
9	255.15		9	0.32
10	283.50		10	0.35
11	311.80		15	0.53
12	340.20		20	0.71
13	368.55		30	1.06
14	396.90		40	1.41
15	425.25		50	1.77
16	453.60		60	2.12
24	679.20		70	2.47
32	907.20		80	2.82
48	1360.80		90	3.18
64	1814.40		100	3.53
100	2834.90			

POUNDS	KG	KG	POUNDS
1	0.45	1	2.20
2	0.91	2	4.41
3	1.36	3	6.61
4	1.81	4	8.82
5	2.27	5	11.02
6	2.72	6	13.23
7	3.18	7	15.43
8	3.63	8	17.64
9	4.08	9	19.84
10	4.54	10	22.05
20	9.07	20	44.09
30	13.61	30	66.14
40	18.14	40	88.18
50	22.68	50	110.23
60	27.22	60	132.27
70	31.75	70	154.32
80	36.29	80	176.36
90	40.82	90	198.41
100	45.36	100	220.46
200	90.72	200	440.92
250	113.40	250	551.15
500	226.80	500	1102.30
750	340.19	750	1,653.45
1,000	453.59	1,000	2,204.60

TONS	TONNES	TONNES	TONS
1	1.02	1	0.98
2	2.03	2	1.97
3	3.05	3	2.95
4	4.06	4	3.94
5	5.08	5	4.92
10	10.16	10	9.84
15	15.24	15	14.76
20	20.32	20	19.68
50	50.80	50	49.21
75	76.20	75	73.82
100	101.60	100	98.42

STONES	KG	STONES	KG
1	6.35	11	69.85
2	12.70	12	76.20
3	19.05	13	82.55
4	25.40	14	88.90
5	31.75	15	92.25
6	38.10	16	101.60
7	44.45	17	107.95
8	50.80	18	114.30
9	57.15	19	120.65
10	63.50	20	127.00

LB/SQ IN	N/m²		MPH	KMH
6	0.041		1	1.6
8	0.062		5	8
10	0.068		10	16
12	0.083		15	24
14	0.097		20	32
16	0.110		25	40
18	0.124		30	48
20	0.138		35	56
22	0.152		40	64
24	0.165		45	72
26	0.179		50	80
28	0.193		55	88
30	0.207		60	96
32	0.221		65	104
34	0.234		70	112
36	0.248		75	120
38	0.262		80	128
40	0.277		85	136
42	0.290		90	144
44	0.303		95	152
46	0.317		100	160
48	0.331		105	168

Degrees Fahrenheit (°F) to Degrees Celsius (°C)

°F	°C	°F	°C
1	-17.2	110	43.3
5	-15.0	115	46.1
10	-12.2	120	48.9
15	-9.4	122	50.0
20	-6.7	125	51.7
25	-3.9	130	54.4
30	-1.1	135	57.2
32	0	140	60.0
35	1.7	145	62.8
40	4.4	150	65.5
45	7.2	155	68.3
50	10.0	160	71.1
55	12.8	165	73.9
60	15.6	170	76.7
65	18.3	175	79.4
70	21.1	180	82.2
75	23.9	185	85.0
80	26.7	190	87.8
85	29.4	195	90.5
90	32.2	200	93.3
95	35.0	205	96.1
100	37.8	210	98.9
105	40.6	212	100.0

18 TEMPERATURE

Degrees Celsius (°C) to Degrees Fahrenheit (°F)

°C	°F
0	32.0
1	33.8
5	41.0
10	50.0
15	59.0
20	68.0
25	77.0
30	86.0
35	95.0
40	104.0
45	113.0
50	122.0
55	131.0
60	140.0
65	149.0
70	158.0
75	167.0
80	176.0
85	185.0
90	194.0
95	203.0
100	212.0

19 FRACTIONS AND DECIMALS

	decimal equivalents		decimal equivalents
1	1.0000	1/23	0.0434
1/2	0.5000	1/24	0.0416
1/3	0.3333	1/25	0.0400
1/4	0.2500	1/26	0.0384
1/5	0.2000	1/27	0.0370
1/6	0.1667	1/28	0.0357
1/7	0.1429	1/29	0.0344
1/8	0.1250	1/30	0.0333
1/9	0.1111	1/40	0.0250
1/10	0.1000	1/45	0.0222
1/11	0.0909	1/50	0.0200
1/12	0.0833	1/55	0.0182
1/13	0.0769	1/60	0.0166
1/14	0.0714	1/65	0.0153
1/15	0.0666	1/70	0.0142
1/16	0.0625	1/75	0.0133
1/17	0.0588	1/80	0.0125
1/18	0.0555	1/85	0.0117
1/19	0.0526	1/90	0.0111
1/20	0.0500	1/95	0.0105
1/21	0.0476	1/100	0.0100
1/22	0.0454	1/1000	0.0010

20 FRACTIONS AND PERCENTAGES

	Per cent			Per cent
1	100.00		1/23	4.34
1/2	50.00		1/24	4.16
1/3	33.33		1/25	4.00
1/4	25.00		1/26	3.84
1/5	20.00		1/27	3.70
1/6	16.67		1/28	3.57
1/7	14.29		1/29	3.44
1/8	12.50		1/30	3.33
1/9	11.11		1/40	2.50
1/10	10.00		1/45	2.22
1/11	9.09		1/50	2.00
1/12	8.33		1/55	1.82
1/13	7.69		1/60	1.66
1/14	7.14		1/65	1.53
1/15	6.66		1/70	1.42
1/16	6.25		1/75	1.33
1/17	5.88		1/80	1.25
1/18	5.55		1/85	1.17
1/19	5.26		1/90	1.12
1/20	5.00		1/95	1.11
1/21	4.76		1/100	1.00
1/22	4.54		1/1000	0.10

ARABIC	ROMAN	BINARY
1	I	1
2	II	10
3	III	11
4	IV	100
5	V	101
6	VI	110
7	VII	111
8	VIII	1000
9	IX	1001
10	X	1010
20	XX	10100
30	XXX	11110
40	XL	101000
50	L	110010
100	C	1100100
200	CC	11001000
300	CCC	100101100
400	CD	110010000
500	D	111110100
1,000	$\overline{\text{M}}$	1111101000
5,000	$\overline{\text{V}}$	1001110001000
10,000	$\overline{\text{X}}$	10011100010000
100,000	$\overline{\text{C}}$	11000011010100000

TEMPERATURE

°F	32	68	104	140	176	212
°C	0	20	40	60	80	100

SPEEDS

mph	20	30	40	50	60	70	80
kmh	32	48	64	80	96	112	128

WEIGHT

stones	8	10	12	14	16	18
kg	51	64	76	89	102	114

HEIGHT

feet	3	4	5	6	7
metres	0.9	1.2	1.5	1.8	2.1

First published 2000 by Armadillo Books
An imprint of Bookmart Limited
Desford Road, Enderby
Leicester LE9 5AD
England

Copyright © 2000 Bookmart Limited

ISBN 1-90046-650-3

Printed in Spain